Single and Sixty

A Reflective and Sometimes Humorous Journey of One Woman's Quest to Deal with Divorce Later in Life

by Janie Jurkovich

Learn to change!
embrace change!
Janie J

Single and Sixty: A Reflective and Sometimes Humorous Journey of One Woman's Quest to Deal with Divorce Later in Life

By Janie Jurkovich

Copyright © 2019

Golden Spiral Press ™ is a trademark of Janie Jurkovich

Book Project Management by Beth Bridges, eBridge Marketing

Editing by Michelle Peterson, Exactly Write Online Marketing

Cover Design by Ellie Dote, Ellie Girl Creations

Interior Design and Layout by Bryan Keith Pfeifer

Author Photos by Suzanne Moles, Wattleweb Global Solutions

Photo Editing by Angie Cibis Graphic Design

First Edition: June 2019
Published by Golden Spiral Press
Fresno, California
www.JanieJ.net

"You're braver than you believe,
and stronger than you seem,
and smarter than you think."

A.A. Milne

DEDICATION

This book is dedicated to Thomas E. Granata, Ph.D., whose guidance and encouragement helped me to process and handle the devastation and disappointment I encountered early on in this journey.

CONTENTS

INTRODUCTION

Everyone experiences change in their lives.

All sorts of change; some good, some not-so-good, and some change is downright awful! But we never know what we will become once we go through the change.

Such is my experience of a dissolved marriage after 35 years. I hesitate to use the words "failed marriage," as lasting 35 years is considered a pretty long run by most standards.

I am a diehard.

I don't quit, sometimes to a fault.

When the choice was taken from me, I realized I had received the greatest gift my former spouse could have ever given me - a chance to grow into the person I yearned to be, the woman I was meant to be … the REAL me.

I encourage you to embrace change - for you never know where it will take you!

Chapter 1

The Departure

The shiny, red 1998 Corvette drove off.

The dust settled. My heart did not.

I was left wondering.

Wondering a lot of things, but mostly wondering *WTF?*

Is he serious?

Sure, every married couple has problems; every married couple has ups and downs, especially after nearly 35 years of marriage. But to drive off with your clothes squished in the back of a Corvette to drive all the way from California to Texas.

No talk. No discussion, except "I can't take it anymore."

What kind of immature imbecile does that? Apparently, my husband.

The first few days were wonderful! I could sleep crosswise in the king size bed. I could actually sleep. Sleep long and deep to my heart's content.

No one snoring, burping, farting or throwing all the covers on top of me. No one turning on the light 20 minutes after I'm asleep followed by gargling and then loud noises from the "pot room."

I was so refreshed. It was wonderful.

Then day three hit. I was wondering when he'd come back. A few days away is good for us both. He'll realize what a good thing he had and come back. No hurry. I can wait. No communication. Gosh, he must have arrived by now. I hope he's okay.

A week later...

Yes, surely by now he's had time to think things over and realize what a good cook I've been, how the house is taken care of, the bills are paid (or at least managed with the use of credit cards), and how holidays and birthdays always mean a special meal with family.

I always did the "wifely" duties because I thought it was expected. Mandatory. Whether you worked outside the home or not.

I only learned in the last 10 years or so, that most of my gal friends didn't cook dinner or clean house. I didn't know it was optional. The memo never got to me.

I wasn't nagging. I'd given up and resolved myself that he would never accept responsibility for his family and do his share around the house (or even a fraction thereof) without numerous reminders and list-making on my part. (He wouldn't even cross items off the list if/when he did complete them!)

My counselor (okay, he was a therapist) had told me years before that my spouse would never change, that he had no initiative, and I shouldn't expect him to ever change. My choices were: accept things like this and live with it *or* leave the marriage.

I'm not a quitter, so I kept trying.

Trying to make up for his inadequacies, lack of drive, forgetfulness and whatever excuse he came up with.

Once he had lost his job (again) and still couldn't find time to help a few hours a week around the house despite apparently having plenty of time each day to watch TV and surf the internet and spend most weekends doing any one of five volunteer activities, I got it … he was never going to make time to do the work/chores necessary to maintain a home.

I relented. I gave up. I resolved myself to the fact I had chosen poorly for a mate.

I accepted the ugly truth.

Each weekend after I cleaned the house, I would finish his chores and the ones I would discover were not done from the weeks prior. Then I would do the bookwork – paying bills, balancing the checkbook, etc.

During the week the laundry, ironing, errands, shopping and meal preparation were fit in between working full-time plus.

I quit nagging. I quit list-making. I just did it all to the point of exhaustion.

Now the mention of enjoying enough sleep can be fully understood.

Finally – an email arrived. He had arrived at the home of his neglected 86-year-old Mum. No one cared about her, and he could surely help care for her, get her meds straight, and her hearing aid and dentures working properly, because *he* could get the doctors doing their jobs.

She needed him. Apparently, I did not.

So that was that; he was staying until she died. Mind you, the woman was not terminally ill or even sick.

Not so much as a mention or discussion about moving permanently or leaving a marriage or working out a compromise.

Again, *WTF?* I guess that question was answered – he's not coming back.

Chapter 2

Searching for Answers

*A*gain, my mind was searching for answers. Why doesn't an adult consult their spouse (even when they are mad) about making such a life-changing decision? We could have reached a compromise.

I was used to being alone months at a time during his military service. I was used to doing most of the work at home anyway.

There are solutions; you just have to have a discussion to find them. Not much hope of that!

What could I have done differently?

Lower my standards? Check, done that.

Don't expect much from him? Check, done that.

Take care of things so his life is less stressful? Check, done that.

Take care of planning all holiday events? Check, done that.

Pick up after him? Check, done that.

Clean up after him? Check, done that.

Avoid conflict? Check, done that.

Don't nag? Check, done that.

Plan getaways to the coast for time together? Check, done that.

Go to a marriage counselor? Check, done that.

Tell him I love him every night and then greet him in the morning with a cheery "hello" and kiss? Check, done that.

What else could I have done?

The answer was clear … I had done everything humanly possible to make his life as stress-free as possible. I simply couldn't do any more.

I wasn't mad, just exhausted.

In talking to my therapist, these things came to light: my spouse had not been stepping up as a partner for a long time, you can't make other people change no matter how hard you try, and lastly, most importantly, perhaps I was an "enabler," who enabled him not to help/participate in our lives together because I took care of everything.

Then I remembered all the times I tried to discuss our budget or how to accomplish something or a problem with the kids.

I either got no response, "let's talk about it later," or a promise to take a certain action that never materialized.

Yes, that's why I accepted responsibility for so much … I had to.

I didn't want to be supermom; I wanted a partner, but since he wasn't there mentally, albeit physically, I had no choice but to go it alone. The good news was I was already doing it alone, so how much harder could it be?

Chapter 3

Going It Alone

I was about to find out just how hard it was to go it alone in a big house and property.

First step was mowing the lawn, not your normal neighborhood lawn, but 10,000 square feet of sod fescue. The irrigation system alone cost $10,000, so I wasn't going to rip it up!

The ex used a riding lawn mower to accomplish this 3-hour-a-week task. I'd ridden it before, and it wasn't nearly as much fun as the tractor or loader. It was much too slow for my liking, but I could certainly do it.

Found the mower … sitting outside the two-car shop I designed to keep things neat and tidy and well-cared for. It had seen the wear and tear of a piece of equipment left outside by someone too lazy to park it inside. Hmph!

Next was trying to find the parts necessary to connect the holding baskets to the mower. It looked like a bolt or two was missing. Checked the manual and everywhere outside and in the shop for the parts. Nothing.

Why can't an adult put something away properly?

I even remember mentioning this to him. So I went to the John Deere dealer to inquire about parts. They looked at the schematic, and I pointed to the parts that seemed to be missing. Waited a few days and made a trip back to the dealer.

Alas, still another piece seemed to be missing. Back again. Fitting in these extra errands to the other side of town between working and other tasks was hard enough, but if I didn't do it soon, the grass would be a foot tall.

Finally, all the pieces were put on to connect the baskets. The gas tank was filled, the oil checked, and the tires were okay. I was ready to mow, well except for figuring out the timing for when to release the mower and engage the PTO (power take off, the thing that makes the blades turn that actually cut the grass).

Whew! I managed to cut the grass, empty the baskets and unclog the shoot several times just to finish mowing the grass once! And that was just the backyard.

Then there was the front yard … what an experience!

Apparently the three large cottonwood trees had grown extensive surface roots that were so bad, it felt like riding an amusement ride at the fair.

Bumpity bump, bumpity bump. This was not so good on my back. Visions of another back surgery came to mind.

All I can say is, I felt an immense sense of accomplishment after it was done. Granted, I took the long route to get the deed done, but it was done. Well, except that is, for the edging; but that's another story.

I managed to mow a couple of times, but it became too much with all the other upkeep. My son finally came to help. Not sure if it was guilt or the money I paid him, but at least he did the mowing.

Next we had to tackle the edging before the grass grew into the landscape beds. I couldn't even get the edger started. I knew enough to check the fluids, but I couldn't pull the cord hard enough to start it.

Once again, guilt prevailed to sway the son to help "poor old mom." He could start the edger, but manipulating it to actually cut where you wanted was quite another thing. It's one of those things that's actually much harder than it looks.

He wasn't very good at it. We decided just to edge every other week. But weeks kept getting missed due to busy schedules, more pressing tasks, etc.

You get it … this was not a glamorous task.

I tried it for a couple weeks when son could start the edger for me and then cut the grass elsewhere in the yard. I felt the sense of his frustration. It took some practice to cut where you actually wanted to cut. The trees in the beds were in the way. And those damn corners.

It was a chore!

Son had school work to do in addition to his real, paid job. I had work to do to earn money to pay for the place or it wouldn't matter if the grass was cut and edged.

Finally, I hired a gardener to mow and edge.

It was expensive (I thought); definitely more expensive than the son's cut-rate, guilt-ridden charges, even though I negotiated less than the gardener originally quoted.

I had no idea how I could afford this new expense, but I did it anyway.

Oh, the freedom to do more important work, and the release of all that frustration, the son who actually looked forward to coming over again. AND the lawn looked FABULOUS! All seemed worth it. Now to the next thing …

There's a golf cart in the shop.

No, it's not used for golfing. It's used to cart around the hula hoe, rake, shovel, pruners and bins while doing yard work around the house. It's a big yard, so it's a necessity to get all that needs to be done, well, done.

I first approached the cart with the intent to load all the garbage, recycle and green waste bins to take them out to the larger bins by the street for trash pick–up the following day. Since this was traditionally the husband's job, I had neglected to do so the first two weeks after his departure.

The 6:00 a.m. roar of the third truck going down the street accompanied by my two dogs barking and running along the front perimeter served as a reminder. It would be impossible to get out there quick enough once the commotion occurred (imagine being in PJs on the second floor, running to the shop, loading the bins, and driving the golf cart to the street, all in a timely manner). No, that wouldn't work.

The garbage department would be finished with the whole neighborhood by the time I was prepared.

Better idea – set "take out trash" on my phone for a weekly reminder! This was a necessity to avoid being overstocked with garbage and items to recycle everywhere.

So the timing was solved, but not the equipment.

I eyed the flat tire. How hard can that be? There's a piece of equipment in the shop that pumps up stuff like bicycle tires, pool rafts, and, I guess, golf cart tires. I think it's called a compressor. So, I tried to figure out how to use it. No "on" and "off" switches.

Where's the manual? After looking in the shop cabinets and drawers and even the filing cabinets in the house, it was located. After a couple read-throughs and getting shocked because the 220-volt cord was frayed, I managed to start it.

Helluva noise!!

Pulled the tightly-wound hose to the tire, unscrewed the valve cap and tried to attach it to the stem on the tire. A couple tries later, it was connected. No gauge to tell when it was full, but, hey, it looked good and felt hard. Turned off the condenser, rewound the hose, put the cap back on the stem, and put the trash out front.

No problem, right? Except for the 20 minutes or so spent fixing the tire when I was supposed to be doing something else, like paying bills or fixing dinner.

The next day I went out to check the tractor in the back acreage with the use of the golf cart, and guess what? The tire was flat again on the golf cart. I repeated the previous procedure with the same results.

OK, now I have to do something more drastic like get the tire fixed, so I'll need to remove it, right? Found the manual (good first step).

Instructions said, "Remove the tire from the axle." I kid you not! The "how" part was unfortunately missing.

Even though my feminist side didn't like asking for help, I relented because I was totally at a loss on what to do next. So I enlisted the help of a friendly neighbor, Joe, who knew how to remove the tire since he was a pro at working on cars.

He showed me what to do as I didn't know there was a hubcap (covering the bolts) and then the bolts had to be removed, but, of course, not until the golf cart was jacked up on one side with, of all things, "a jack." I wondered what that tool and the two stands were for. Now was my chance to figure it out.

Tire removed. Voilà!

Put it in the trunk and drove to the tire shop for a "free" repair, which was only moderately comforting, given the chore to get the tire there in the first place. I kind of felt like they should be paying me for all my efforts.

And to think, when it was repaired later that day, I got to reverse the chore (albeit without the help of friendly neighbor Joe).

Note to self – don't wear white pants to work on days you are likely to be sidetracked changing a tire.

But the tire fiasco proved to be a very good lesson as it was to occur many times over the next several months. I found out other helpful tips, too: don't drive off the regular nicely scraped paths (nicely scraped by myself on the tractor), lest you want a puncture vine to give you more flat tires, AND there is this green goo you can insert in the tire to fill holes so you don't have to go to the tire shop so often. It doesn't require a jack and stands either, so all the more helpful.

This country life was a snap.

I wanted to enjoy the outdoors and beautiful sunrises and sunsets … too bad I missed another sunset tending to another new emergency on a regular basis!

At one point there were so many things that kept requiring repairs that it was totally overwhelming. I remember sitting in my car in the garage and yelling out loud to God that if this was a sign that I needed a man in my life to fix things, I was not going to give in; I would not quit!

After that, there were still many challenges to be dealt with on a regular basis, but I felt like I had weathered the storm and gotten the hang of it.

This next incident exemplifies my epiphany of how to deal with these unfortunate episodes or "growing experiences" as others might refer to them.

It started out a great day.

At 5:30 a.m. I was enjoying a cup of coffee on the balcony watching the sun rise, gazing off at the scenery – the neighbor's pond and the grazing cows, and then my own yard until …

Wow! What's that geyser in the backyard? Oh, crap, another busted sprinkler.

Off I go to the backyard to turn off the sprinklers and retrieve the sprinkler head. I tried to screw it on, and the darn thing was too wet. I needed a rag to dry it off. I looked back to the house and thought, "no time and too far."

So I took off my nightgown (ala Gone with the Wind style – if you remember the scene with Melanie and the dead soldier), used it to dry the sprinkler head, reattached it, and put my wet nightgown back on. Voilà! It was fixed. Now I could get ready for work.

I thought, damn, I do NOT want to do that again.

This was the third repair within a week, although the other repairs didn't require such drastic action. I am NOT, repeat, NOT doing this again.

It's not that I can't do it or I won't do it. It is not because it frustrates the heck out of me when I've got a million other things to do. It's because it's not the best use of my time!

Someone else could do it better and faster and relieve me of my misery.

So ... within a week, I hired a qualified sprinkler repairman who loves repairing sprinklers and is much better at it than I. He has made several trips since then, too.

I thought about all the frustrations of running a country home and managing several commercial buildings and trying to work as a real estate broker.

If you throw in construction inspections and sitting on a board as secretary and CFO, no wonder I felt like I had no time to do my "real" job.

We've all heard it over and over: delegate. My trusted administrative assistant had been a godsend since I expanded my company's focus from property management to leasing properties, yet I had resisted further "staff" or helpers.

But this time, I was desperate.

I admitted that I just couldn't do it all.

Then I hired a maintenance worker to repair stuff at home and at the properties. I hired someone else to run errands (3-4 hours a week).

It was amazing. In just the second week, I had time to actually "think" instead of making knee-jerk reactions to the latest emergency. I was able to complete assignments, some of which had been waiting weeks!

Next, I hired someone to help with the yard, officially called an Outdoor Laborer, to do all the routine and sometimes heavy yard work. I was off to a good start!

All these "helpers" were part-time or "as needed," so although it was an added expense, it freed up my time to do my work and helped me retain my sanity (priceless).

Even after hiring more staff to help around the house and at the properties, my challenges or "learning experiences" continued.

One such event was changing the bulbs at the front gate. They were out, so I bought matching frosted, tipped bulbs with the small ends. Who knew there were so many styles? Changed bulbs and waited 'til evening when the photocell comes on.

No lights … what's going on??

Asked my new maintenance guy to try to figure it out as I wanted to avoid a more expensive electrician and possibly ordering new light fixtures. I didn't want to go down that road. After he worked on the problem, he let me know that the sockets where the bulbs fit were full of little dead bugs – gnats or something – which prevented the bulbs from making full contact. Once he blew or brushed the bugs away, the bulbs worked properly.

Voilà! The lights were "on" at the gate the next time I returned home after an evening at a networking event!

More than once the electrician David, a dear friend by then, came to the house to address electrical issues. I tried trouble-shooting myself first, as I am (I'm embarrassed to say) a licensed general contractor, albeit a "paper contractor." That means I hire subcontractors and oversee their work versus actually doing any work.

He routinely replaced electrical outlets where the GFIs kept blowing and sprinkler clocks and outdoor lights failed to ignite. The two service calls that really blew my mind were because some entry lights kept getting dimmer and dimmer, and I could barely see at night when I turned them on. Did you catch that word "dimmer?" That should have been my clue.

A dimmer switch had been installed as a result of building code energy-efficiency changes and improvements, and apparently the cleaning crew moved the switch, and all that was required was to slide the dimmer switch up all the way. It was a very expensive lesson … and one I shall not make again!

Another time after Mom's dog peed (again) in the living room, I had the carpet cleaning guy come all the way out to the house to clean one room of carpeting. He left the ceiling fan on to help dry out the carpeting.

A few days later I checked the carpet, which was fine, but the fan was already turned off, which I hadn't done. I tried to turn it back on. Off. On. Off. On. Several times. No luck.

Visions of replacing the entire fixture danced in my head. This fan was a bit fancier than most, and I had originally located it and ordered it online, not like the other fans throughout the house, which were purchased from a local hardware store.

Another electrician service call …

This time the switch on the fan that changes direction of the blades was positioned in the middle so it wouldn't move either way. Apparently, this was a result of dusting the fan when the cleaning crew recently visited.

Another expensive lesson that wouldn't happen again. On the bright side, it didn't involve ordering and installing a new fan, and I was helping the electrician keep food on his table.

Like I said, look at the bright side.

Chapter 4

The Ring

My friend Kay, whom I met at several of my networking groups, explained she was selling her jewelry collection. Not her personal collection, but one she'd been selling as her means of employment.

I remember seeing a catalog of this jewelry a few months back because I took the catalog home and perused it over and over again with coffee in the morning, trying to decide which pieces to purchase.

Alas, after a few weeks I decided I'd better toss the catalog, lest I purchase them all. To say the line of jewelry was beautiful was an understatement.

So imagine my glee when Kay mentioned she was selling her stock. I even brought my mom (who already owns enough jewelry to open a small store). We went to Kay's house on the appointed day.

So many pieces, never enough money, what a choice to make!

I purchased a gorgeous black and diamond necklace/bracelet pair that would set off any "Little Black Dress," something that would definitely come in handy.

Doesn't that resemble a "justification" for a purchase?

But the pièce de résistance was a huge diamond ring. It had a large, very large, rectangular diamond in the middle. Each side had three rows of three diamonds. It was so over the top that it was almost gaudy.

I say "almost" gaudy because once I put it on my finger – it was not gaudy, but magnificent! I've never had such an instantaneous connection to a piece of jewelry, especially one that was not practical like the LBD pieces, but an utter splurge (something I'd never had).

Thank God the price didn't break the bank, and my mother, the quintessential shopper, even agreed I should buy it.

There was one additional interesting tidbit … the ring in all its magnificence, only fit on my left ring finger, not the right hand. Thirty-five years of bondage had made the ring finger on the left hand noticeably smaller. There was no way this rock was going to fit on the other hand – it was too small. This was the only size available as this was a close-out sale.

I must say it was "kismet" that the ring only fit on the site of my former wedding ring.

I understood the meaning … I was married to myself.

Not in some narcissistic way, but in a way that says, "I love who I am, just the way I am. I can take care of myself, and I don't need a man, thank you very much!"

I can't tell you how energized, proud, and confident it made me feel to wear that ring. It was so enormous; no one could miss it but a blind person. It was heavy enough that I even noticed it without looking at it.

The cost was well worth it because it was the start of a new chapter of self-sufficiency.

Chapter 5

The "Do Over"

*I*t's all about attitude.

Instead of thinking about what I had lost and having a pity party, I decided to look at my situation in a different way.

In politics they call it "spinning," but we can do this in our own lives as well!

I looked at my marriage in terms of what I gained versus what I lost.

I had had the opportunity to travel to other countries and states, to be employed in many different jobs, meet new people and experience other cultures. I grew to be independent because he was gone so much for his work. I grew to be strong and versatile. We experienced the blessing of adopting our son!

All these things happened because I was with my ex. I had an adventure that I wanted at the time. I received exactly what I desired.

"Don't be sad, be happy," I told myself numerous times.

Without the grumpy guy around, there was much more room in

bed. I could sleep sideways and eat in bed with no complaints. I could hog the covers and turn the electric blanket up real high or not at all. I could listen to music as I drifted off to sleep. (Music that I wouldn't even be allowed to play if he was here.) I could even sleep 'til noon with no interruptions.

What joy! What bliss!

All those chick flicks on TV that I couldn't watch due to someone monopolizing the TV and my limited free time, were now mine to enjoy to my heart's content. Documentaries on health, well-being, spirituality, and even Oprah's Super Soul Sunday, were mine for the taking.

Again, what joy! What bliss!

And music ... OMG being able to listen to Yanni, Il Divo, Celine Dion and other "new" artists from 10 years ago that I had never discovered before.

It was amazing!

Their music was uplifting, powerful, sensitive, sensual and generally "feel-good." I could listen all day long. Really loud. Whatever I chose.

What a relief!

No rude comments that dampened my mood. Just joy and passion. Whoohoo!

Yes, the relationship was over. I did my best and I couldn't change someone else.

Repeat to self: I really can't change someone else, especially if they don't want to change.

Remind self: Be thankful because this gives me the opportunity to find true love – someone who will love me back, the way I deserve to be loved!

I truly believe that!! And if I am wrong, so be it, but I know what I deserve.

New opportunities were now on the horizon.

I had the chance to make my own fun – movies with friends, travel, concerts, wine-tasting and being out and about with positive, uplifting friends.

Enjoying life. What a treat!

I reminded myself – this new life was only possible because my marriage had ended.

Chapter 6

Finances

*Y*es, that dirty word that consumes most of the waking hours of humankind.

How do I pay for what I want, need and cherish in life?

Or more importantly, how do I survive?

One day early in our separation, I was in my home office trying to figure out what to do.

My life as I'd known it for 35 years was in shambles. I was an emotional wreck. I didn't know if we'd work things out and he'd be back within a month or I'd never see him again.

Finances especially were a real worry.

I didn't really make that much money. I couldn't sell the house. I'd sunk all the cash from my inheritance into my dream home.

I was lucky in one way; my ex still had his military retirement check going to a joint account and I had access to the account. But there was uncertainty as to when/if he might change the military allotment to another account that only he had access to.

Then the Great Recession hit. My home was now worth $400,000 less than what it cost to build! I couldn't lose it. Besides, I loved living there.

After years of moving around the world for the military, I finally had a place I designed, built and figured out how to pay for. I just couldn't lose it.

I needed this place like I needed air.

No, there must be an answer, and the most immediate need was coming up shortly because the house payment and line of credit were due. Yikes!

I was sitting at my desk in my home office, in my pajamas, crying and worrying, when I looked at my calendar. I had an appointment in less than an hour with a networking friend and there was no way in hell I was going to be ready and get to his office in time.

Let alone be emotionally prepared.

I called him and blurted out that I couldn't make the meeting to discuss our businesses, something required by this new networking group I had joined.

I explained my husband had left, I was an emotional mess and still in my pajamas at 10:00 am. He said, "Don't worry, we can reschedule."

Two minutes later, Robin, an attorney from the same networking group, called me (she was actually the one who suggested I join).

She very sternly told me to get to the bank immediately and open another account, only in my name, and transfer all the funds to it. She said to use it to pay all joint bills going forward.

"Don't use it for anything else," she instructed. "You must do it right now."

She was really bossy and insistent, not like her usually calm and laid-back self. She said even if we get back together, this will still be OK.

"You have to protect yourself," she insisted.

I figured it must be urgent, so I got dressed and did as she instructed.

In my case it turned out not to be an issue. Or maybe that's because I had opened this separate account.

My ex deferred to my handling of joint expenses as he had during our marriage, but I'm sure many women have been left out in the cold because they didn't take these quick, proactive measures.

Lessons learned: protect yourself financially as quick as you can and seek legal advice if you even have an inkling things are going south.

The other lesson is never underestimating the power and influence of friends. They are here to help you and guide you when you need it most.

I know I was very lucky. I had only recently joined this networking group. Yet they had my back while I made this journey. Many of the folks (both men and women) are still close friends. We've grown and helped each other in business and personal decisions.

Thank God for friends!

Chapter 7

Income from Work

So the income from his military retirement was handled for now, but I would still need more money to pay the full house payment, to maintain the house, pay utilities and buy groceries.

It was time to double down on the income-making.

I had already learned to delegate some household chores, so I needed to do the same at work. My assistant started handling more tasks that I previously was doing.

I hired another real estate agent to learn the business. I focused more on "real deals" in the business – the ones that had a reasonable chance of succeeding.

I had to learn how to say, "Sorry, I can't help you," and suggest something else for those seeking assistance.

I had to change my mindset from being responsible for helping every person who called to the realization that time is money in the real estate business.

Time is all I have to use to make money, and I need to be as efficient as possible and realistic about whether or not I can help people and make any commission.

At first it felt cold and calculating to think of a transaction this way. But advice from other agents helped me to view things more realistically.

As mothers and wives, we are taught to take care of others and basically not get "paid."

We're used to being devalued.

We want to help. We want to make it "all better."

The guys in commercial real estate gave me a wake-up call. Basically, they told me, "You're not going to make it in this business unless you sort through the wheat from the chaff and work real deals. You'll starve if you don't."

OK, time to step up and play with the big boys. Once again, luckily, I had a network of agents to ask questions. Every bit of info they passed on to me was gleaned and adopted.

It was time to work smarter, not harder, or I'd drown myself in exhaustion.

I wrote out questionnaires and checklists to discuss with potential clients. I knew which questions to ask on the first phone call to even decide if it was worth meeting with them. When presenting properties, I gave clients as much info as possible to lead to decisions quicker.

I learned the fine art of the follow-up. If you checked back too quickly or too often, you became a nuisance. If you didn't follow up often enough, they went elsewhere.

I made all the mistakes and learned from them.

I used my experience as a building owner, property manager, contractor, and real estate agent to look at deals from every side's perspective. I actively shared this with clients so they could understand how the owner felt.

I focused on the type of commercial transactions I wanted to do. No office, no retail, just industrial.

I set alerts with the property listing service for new listings in my preferred size range. I drove by industrial areas and kept abreast of my little part of the market. The synergy that developed made deals seamless. Inquiring parties would call, and I could tell them the addresses, square footage and lease rates off the top of my head.

I set my intention and focus. This kept me afloat. Business was good. My properties were all leased. I helped other owners.

My income increased and I was secure enough for now.

Chapter 8

Shoot that Squirrel!

When I first saw a squirrel in the garden area, he stopped and looked at me and ran back to the yard. I thought, "How cute."

Little did I know the havoc the critters would wreak in the backyard. They dug tunnels under the rocks behind the pool where the waterfall was. They even got in the drain pipes in the landscape bed and pushed off the lids.

Then they dug underground like 200' to the electric subpanel by the shop. The electricity went to the shop and backyard. This was serious. They could cause a lot of damage.

To top it off, in the morning when I sat on the balcony enjoying the sun, I could see them sunbathing on the rocks! One, two, three, four, five of those damn squirrels.

It was time for action, but what?

I purchased two cages to trap animals and set them up behind the pool where they lived. I used birdseed as bait. I checked the traps in the morning and afternoon.

Nothing.

One day when a GF came over to swim and sunbathe, I ventured behind the pool, not expecting anything. But I caught one! Not a very convenient time for me as I had company.

I set him aside nearby so we could keep an eye on him. Just before sunset, I took the cage to neighbor Joe, the one who helped with the golf cart tire. He took care of the critter and returned the cage to me. One down, four to go.

This procedure kept happening, and I was making progress. Fewer of them to taunt me on the rocks in the morning.

One day there was a cute little black and white critter in the cage, also known as a baby skunk. I wasn't moving the cage this time!

I called the neighbor; he came over and took care of the skunk while I stayed on the other side of the rocks. I couldn't bear to watch.

When I returned to the cage, I looked at the collapsed and dead skunk. I looked at Joe. No one moved.

Okay, I guess I can't expect him to pull it out of the cage, too.

I picked up the cage and dumped out the skunk. Pause. Again, no reaction from Joe, he just looked at me. I used a plastic bag and picked up the skunk. Yikes!

"Did I really pick up a dead skunk?" I asked myself.

It was placed in another bag and tied. Joe said, "We're supposed to bury them, not put them in the trash." (There's your disclaimer, Joe.)

I said, "The ground is like concrete out here and I don't have time to dig a hole!"

Into the garbage bin, carefully covered, he went.

Only one or two more squirrels were caught – and then eventually, all five. But the problem remained, and I couldn't figure out why until I saw squirrel #6 sunbathing in the morning.

Damn! That one was still eluding me.

He had been digging near the electrical lines, but, thankfully, no more damage in the landscape bed behind the pool.

One day I saw him out there, grabbed a pellet gun and went out to "get" him. He scampered away while I yelled obscenities at him.

But, I do know when I catch the remaining squirrel, there will be no more calling the neighbor. It is time to stand on my own.

There will continue to be more rodent challenges ahead, but I feel ready to meet them!

Chapter 9

Connecting with Girlfriends

What an important element!

I never really had the opportunity to build female friendships due to frequent military moves, job changes and family/work commitments. This had been a missing component in my life.

Fortunately, during the last five years, I had started cultivating female friendships once I needed to expand my business beyond managing and building family-owned buildings.

I recognized the need to network, but for me networking meant women's groups as I was too intimidated for the "big league" (i.e. groups that included men).

By attending various monthly meetings, seeing some of the same ladies at multiple meetings, I started to feel confident enough to have discussions beyond work-related issues.

Then, after attending a session at the local women's conference regarding friendships and how to cultivate them and grow them, I realized there is actually a method to it.

I couldn't understand why I felt closer to some people and others seemed disinterested in forming friendships. But the speaker, Shasta Nelson, helped me recognize there are different types of friendships and it takes conscious effort to move a "friend" up the chain to "best buddy" status (read her book, *Friendships Don't Just Happen!: The Guide to Creating a Meaningful Circle of Girlfriends* for more).

I recognized which women friends I wanted to get to know better and made conscious attempts to do so. They didn't all work out, but many efforts led to a group of ladies I could turn to for emotional support and guidance when needed. Even a stern talking-to, when needed, was something I was grateful for.

Seriously, I don't know how I would have managed without some sort of support group from various girlfriends.

It was great to have some "pals" to do fun activities with, too. I hate to admit it, but I had led a rather sheltered life, mostly concentrating on work and family. There was no time for friends.

Thankfully, only due to work requirements, this had recently changed. Now, I knew a few friends to go to the movies, out to lunch or shopping. A couple times we went to a local winery for wine tasting.

Just getting out was mood-lifting.

This led to bigger ideas such as a trip to Portugal with a girlfriend.

We tagged along with a local chamber of commerce for a great, stress-free, fun, memory-making trip.

What a joy to go someplace I'd always wanted to go and learn about another culture, their history and their food!

One day I stayed at the hotel, skipping the tour of a cork factory and beautiful countryside. Instead, I spent the day at the beach and the three conjoined swimming pools while indulging in a pitcher of sangria and a romance novel.

What a life!

When the other tourmates returned late in the day, all haggard and weary, I was refreshed, recently showered and enjoying a drink at the bar. I felt rejuvenated and rested. Something I hadn't been in a very long time.

This would only be possible with the encouragement of girlfriends and the willingness to dream big and step out of my everyday life.

Figuring out a way to pay for the trip was a minor, although important, part of the trip. The big factor was just deciding to do something so outrageous and out of my solid work-ethic mode. But it was definitely one of my best decisions!

I learned to trust myself that I could find a way to do things I had always wanted.

Another girlfriend and I went for a quick trip to France. We enjoyed a whirlwind visit to Paris and Nice in southern France. We made our own arrangements.

It was quite an "adventure," definitely something I wouldn't have done if still married. We found ways to cut costs and cover our expenses, proving if there's a will, there's a way.

Chapter 10

Self-Care

This was a term I was only recently familiar with.

It means taking care of yourself, something that we women, as wives and mothers, seldom do. It is SO important to do this.

I sincerely wish someone would have told me the importance of self-care earlier in my life.

I would have been in a much better place emotional and physically going into this divorce.

I focused on taking care of myself, little by little. Those visits to the manicurist were written in my planner just like a business meeting. Pedicures were even occasionally included.

The bliss that followed a scheduled massage!

The hour-long walk with a friend in early morning. Signing up for paint classes and enforced "relaxation and learning" experiences. Just taking the time to look outside and write a poem in the morning was wonderful.

Learning to play golf, hit golf balls with friends and participating in a tournament were welcomed outlets. Taking a lunch break to lay out by the pool, soak up the sun and listen to soft music, was totally rejuvenating.

Taking a couple minutes to dance in the driveway when I returned from the gym in the early morning, complete with the car stereo blaring, was such fun!

The focus of self-care is to create *happiness*.

Once I figured out what made me happy, truly happy, I found ways to incorporate these moments into my everyday life.

What a difference it made in my outlook and ability to cope with the challenges of life, especially going through such a major life change.

Chapter 11

A State of Stagnation

*T*hings were not moving along though for the divorce, despite prodding from my ex. I had somehow become the one responsible for getting the divorce done (do you see a pattern here of shifting responsibilities?). For me, it was overwhelming, frustrating, and time-consuming.

This led to a discussion with my therapist.

I candidly asked him, "Why am I not getting the divorce paperwork finished? Why does it keep being put on the back burner after other emergencies?"

He said it was simple. Doing divorce paperwork is not a pleasant task, and it doesn't make any money (which I desperately needed). It was normal.

A sense of relief fell over me. So THAT was why.

But a few weeks later, I was still struggling to finish the deed.

A good friend struck the nail on the head. We were having a frank discussion about why I hadn't finished reviewing the documents from the paralegal so we could move closer to finalizing the divorce.

"I'm just too busy with work, you know. Every day has serious emergencies, and I must keep up with clients so I can make money to survive," I said.

She looked me straight in the eyes and said, "You are mourning the loss of your marriage."

I teared up.

That hadn't occurred to me.

I was 25 years old when we married and I was married to him for 35 years.

I had been married more years than my whole life prior to marriage!

No wonder it felt like losing a limb, albeit one with gangrene. A limb that you know must be removed if you are to live. It was solace!

I was prompted to go home and review the paperwork for an hour and a half that night. I might add this woman was such a good friend that she texted me in the evening to gently remind me of what I needed to do.

Chapter 12

The "Shift" Occurring

I took to heart my therapist's and financial advisor's and friend's advice:

It is NOT your job to worry about *him*. It's your job to think about the future. When thoughts go to the past, about what could have been, redirect them to the FUTURE.

This is a learned response.

Deliberate action must be taken until the brain naturally, automatically, thinks of the future and my new life ahead.

It sounds like this in my head:

STOP, PIVOT, REDIRECT → FUTURE

STOP, PIVOT, REDIRECT → FUTURE → HAPPY

HAPPY, CALM, AT PEACE → READY TO MOVE ON

I'M READY.

Well, at least I'll keep telling myself it's so until it is reality!

It was time to stop riding the "Regret Train" as my therapist called it. When I started thinking about how life should have been or could have been with him – I tried so hard to redirect my thoughts and think about the future instead of the past and what was lost. It took several months to finally come to terms.

Then one weekend as I was watching Oprah's Super Soul Sunday, it suddenly became super clear!

Dr. Brené Brown said, "Grief is embedded in forgiveness," and "You need to grieve first to be able to forgive."

I had to grieve my vision or dream of a loving relationship that did not occur. I had to be sad first. Then I could move on to forgiveness and let go of the anger.

Just be sad that he can't, won't or isn't capable of fulfilling those needs in either of us.

It was finally time.

Time to cut the cord. I sat quietly and envisioned a cord connecting us, belly to belly. It had certainly felt like we were connected after all those years together.

In my mind, I took a big pair of blue scissors and cut the imaginary cord.

It was over. Finito. The end.

It's sad, but things do happen for a reason, and I do believe life will be much better in the future.

Learning life's lessons is often hard and difficult to bear. But I knew once I got through it – it would be a cleansing experience.

Chapter 13

Deciding to _Really_ Move Ahead

OK, I'll admit it.

After getting it together and meeting with the financial advisor and reviewing all the assets, I went home and thought, "This doesn't make sense. I need to review this again when I'm clear headed and can concentrate."

Alas, it sat on my desk (or the table next to my desk where all the "to do" list items sit until I can manage them).

First there were appointments with the CPA about the possible sale of property.

Then meetings with a real estate broker about the value of said property.

The tax consequences, the final result and trying to figure out if selling was even a viable option.

My brain was overwhelmed with facts, figures, and gut feelings.

Then there were meetings with an attorney regarding property affected by an eminent domain issue from the state.

Sure, our building was saved, but at the cost of severely affecting our capacity to lease it and make money the way it was originally built. Questions arose – how can we make this property work and still make money? Is the money we are being offered going to be sufficient to cover our expenses? Will we lose our tenants in the meantime?

Meet with an appraiser. Meet with a Civil Engineer. Complete several forms for all five owners, which require consulting with attorney and accountant. Obtaining all signatures and additional documents and submitting them to the proper agency.

My head was spinning with all these decisions and tasks to do.

In the meantime, there were issues at home – front gate won't open, garage door won't close, washing machine sounds like a roll of pennies were deposited, the dogs are going nuts when the neighboring waterpark sets off fireworks, and then they commence to chew the trim off the door.

To say things were again overwhelming was an understatement!

There were meetings with tenants about renewing their leases, as well as keeping tabs on current real estate transactions and responding to questions from owners and potential clients.

Oh my, I took a deep breath.

Life in general was getting to be too much! Working later didn't help.

It just meant no dinner until 11:00 p.m. when a bowl of cereal would suffice and missed morning workouts due to exhaustion. After working late, the extra sleep was a necessity.

I kept telling myself it will get better, and I kept plugging along.

Talks with friends and their encouragement helped immensely. Sessions with the therapist helped. Finally, after prodding by my ex, I found time to settle down and review the financials. They didn't make sense any longer. Too many questions. I made another appointment with the financial advisor.

Three hours later I grasped an understanding of it all: we must split all retirement accounts. If I get the house, I have to pay out his equity. We still need money to pay our debts.

Okay, I understood it all, but knew I would soon forget the details in my brain filled with a million other important details.

I resolved to "trust myself" and just tell myself it's right so I wouldn't keep rehashing it over in my mind.

I couldn't take the stress and feelings of overwhelment to be repeated.

OK – it's done.

I have to come up with a bunch of money and lose assets, but we will both be "okay" in our upcoming retirement years. Now I just have to tell the ex and try to explain it to him.

The financial advisor said she could explain it to him if I was unable to do so.

I just might have to take her up on it.

The next step was working with an attorney to iron out the details legally. Thank goodness for all those networking groups where I met a reasonable attorney who focused on divorce mediation.

No need for the excessive barracuda lawyer who would suck him and any remaining assets dry.

No sense squeezing the turnip. He'd suffered enough, and I just couldn't drag him through the mud.

It wouldn't make *me* feel any better to see him suffer.

The high road is better, and the result would be the same, just at a higher emotional and financial cost.

It was time to move on. Ready or not. Happy or not.

Time to just get it done!

Emotionally done – check.

Financially done – check.

Legally done – check.

Get over it already!

Janie Jurkovich

Chapter 14

Dating Ups and Downs

After much, and I mean much, encouragement and pushing from friends, I relented and joined a popular online dating site.

For someone off the market for over 35 years, it was quite a shock!

Sure, I'd heard all about these sites – how everybody and their brother found true love just a few clicks away.

I decide to jump in the game.

I carefully drafted a bio and description of what I was looking for, including the remarks "no couch potatoes" or anyone ready for retirement.

I was looking for a guy ready to get up and go, do things, travel, play golf, something, anything but watch TV on the boob tube.

I expanded the search from 55 to 65, even though I felt any guys my age or older were too old but then I quickly realized any men near the age of 60 were set on women under 50.

Only retired guys with too much time on their hands replied.

They obviously didn't read the "not ready for retirement" part of my entry.

I wanted to spread my wings and fly, something I hadn't done in a very long time. I couldn't remember the last time my ex and I even went out on a date.

I wanted to make up for the lost time!

It was interesting to run across guys I knew from business. I didn't know they were available and looking.

This wasn't exactly in my repertoire of business conversations: "What's your business? Where are you located? ... Are you free on Friday night?"

Nope that's not how I operate.

In fact, I don't "operate" in any sort of fashion. Maybe that's the problem. Nevertheless, I found it very disheartening to find guys I knew who were my age on a dating site looking for young babes as trophy wives.

Maybe I should look for a "trophy husband."

You know, a guy who looks great, is great in the sack, but you don't really have a real relationship with.

Once or twice I actually found such a prospect on the dating site.

Not to miss out, I quickly sent a note to the guy whose picture looked like it was out of a fashion magazine and whose bio was even more intriguing … complete with a romantic Italian name.

He responded quickly in broken English and sounded interesting. But poof! He was quickly offline.

Most likely being kicked off the site, for inappropriate behavior, like asking women to contact him directly.

Oh well, one can only dream.

Another annoying observance was all the pictures of guys with their fish.

OK, we're supposed to include pics of our favorite activities, and I realize a photo of a guy with a remote in his hand, eating popcorn and belching is not going to score a hot chick.

But, really, how many fish do you need to show us women?

This wasn't the Sportsman.com dating site (if there even is one)! [Editors note: there are many.]

I'm not impressed with the size of your fish. It doesn't translate into any manly status to me.

Sure, I do like to fish, but pics of guys holding a fish, dressed in grubbies with a three-day beard don't look particularly promising to me. If that's the best you can do, I think I'll pass.

I tried another dating site and realized you had to actually be divorced. Dang! Oh well, at least it keeps the married guys out. Maybe.

I hadn't even thought about that, but remember I'd been living under a rock.

I checked out another dating site, but my son promptly told me, "No, that's a hook-up site."

"A what?" I questioned.

There is something about having your 29-year-old son tell you what a "hook-up" is that is both shocking and embarrassing. (*You* can check Google for an explanation!)

You mean people really "do that?"

He confirmed that I had been living under a rock.

Dating and society in general, had apparently changed quite a bit during my decades of marriage.

I did sign up for another dating site used solely on my phone. It was a bit more difficult to maneuver due to technical difficulties, mostly on my end (i.e., I didn't know what the hell I was doing). I swiped left when I meant right and vice versa.

This resulted in tossing away the interesting ones and telling the scruffy guy with the beanie I "liked" him. The only redeeming fact was that you only "connected" if the guy already liked you.

That reminds me, I didn't hear from the "beanie" guy, so even he didn't like me!

It seemed only guys under 60 were able to use this site, so at least it weeded out the older, retired couch potatoes. I know they aren't all couch potatoes, but the active ones are probably out hiking Mt. Kilimanjaro or competing in the 100-mile bike ride in Palm Desert.

The bottom line was, this dating app was new in our area, and few guys were even using it. I'd check daily, and there were literally no guys in my area.

I needed another avenue to meet guys.

I tried networking activities, this time the local chambers of commerce, because unlike the women's groups, there were actually men who attended.

Even having a non-traditional job in commercial real estate and a background in construction, it was difficult to meet anyone who wasn't already married. But it was a great experience to go out and build "people" skills and learn how to talk somewhat intelligently without being so self-conscious and nervous!

One tip I learned early on was to ask them lots of questions. Then you barely have to talk and the other person thinks you're a wonderful conversationalist.

Next up, I searched online to check on old boyfriends. Not that I was trying to rekindle anything, but just to find someone I knew who might go out with me.

The wonder of Google. I found out most men were married.

No surprise there. Some lived too far away. I did find one friend from college who was now living back in the same town. It took a bit of investigative work, but I finally found a phone number and left a message. I was sure he'd call back, so I was hopeful.

Chapter 15

Preparing for Love

*I*n the meantime, after the online dating demoralization, I started thinking about what I could do to look more attractive.

It wasn't just to get a man, that's too barbaric anyway. But it would hopefully increase my confidence, and my natural charm would take over.

No? Well, it was worth a shot.

I decided to pursue the least drastic action that I understand all divorced women resort to first thing … new undergarments.

No more white grandma bloomers.

The only colors in my underwear drawer were white, nude and beige. I was a real fashion guru.

I had always figured, well, they went with everything. There was no need to buy a fancy red bra that only went with one blouse.

No, not me. I was way-too-practical (and cost-conscious) Jane, more likely referred to as 'Plain Jane.'

I decided to throw caution to the wind!

Multiple colors and styles of undies were now in my drawer. They didn't resemble the styles/colors from Victoria Secret, but for me it was a definite step out of the comfort zone into the wild life.

Oh, the same tactic for bras and "shapewear." Some were even in animal prints … oh my!

These changes also emerged in my work and casual clothing. Previously I wore black or white pants and a colored top. It was easier, I reasoned. It was also safer; more businesslike, I reasoned.

That was true, but it was B O R I N G.

I slowly got bolder in my clothing (more colors, more stylish, lower necklines, tighter pants, and more dresses and skirts and even higher heels).

Guess what? It was fun! It increased my confidence, and people noticed, even guys. It made me happier.

I decided to live a little.

Then I checked out the most drastic action: surgery. Figured a boob lift might be in order since the ladies were heading south at an alarming pace.

It was quite shocking, actually.

I figured I could live with a small scar above the breast when the doctor pulled them up 6" where they belonged.

But noooo ... that's not how they do it.

The "fix" requires relocating the nipple, and implants, and a lollipop scar, and, most importantly, you could lose feeling in your breasts.

I'm not going there.

Better to opt for dim lights and a negligee.

I'll be lying down mostly, and most guys over 50 need glasses anyway. Yep, smoke and mirrors versus the knife is the way for me!

What else could I do?

I made a trip to my friend's makeup counter at Macy's (see? I said having girlfriends was key). She taught me about facials, moisturizers, really good makeup and how to apply it.

Another GF showed me her makeup line. We played and practiced.

I bought more makeup. Got bolder. Got better.

Things were improving. I felt more confident.

Working out regularly was another game changer.

Even though I had a gym membership, nothing significant was happening in the physical fitness arena. I was gaining more flexibility and balance at age 60, but still couldn't keep up with 70- and 80-year-olds in my Pilates class.

Swimming helped, but I couldn't afford another hour at the gym to start work at 11:00 am!

I hired a personal trainer and that helped a bit. I lost some weight and got in better shape, but my momentum waned when I missed weeks of workouts due to vacation.

The momentum, as well as the trainer, didn't return.

I tried working out at home – taking baby steps and using charts and discussing these goals with a mastermind group.

Finally, I started an intensive women's bootcamp, and it worked! It's a habit that stuck. It's fun, and the results were amazing.

My confidence soared.

Sexy clothes were fun to wear. It was a definite game changer.

Then I found out the big news: my mom had been tattooed.

No, say it isn't so!

And her sister! I couldn't believe it.

Yes, their eyebrows were tattooed! I had wondered where *my* eyebrows had gone. When I went to the gym in the morning, I had to pencil them in before I could see my face.

A scary sight.

Apparently, they had solved this dilemma by having their eyebrows tattooed.

Since it was rather expensive and I'm too budget-conscious (ok, cheap), my mom paid for my tattoo for my birthday.

Try explaining that one to your son, "Oh yea, Grandma paid for my tattoo, just like hers and Auntie's."

The procedure was painful, even after the numbing medicine was applied. I literally cried. She had to stop frequently and try again. I was officially the "biggest wimp."

But the results were FABULOUS!

I could find my eyes in the morning. Add some lipstick and call it a face. Off to the gym I go.

The beautician, Faye, had said "eyebrows frame your face." They are infinitely more important than eyelashes … a little-known fact.

Next, a visit to my doctor seemed in order. I needed to find out what sort of "preparations" were necessary.

The first preparation I could think of was the lack of a sex drive, to which the doctor promptly prescribed testosterone cream, which did nothing except add another trip to the pharmacy for me.

When I returned, she tested me, TWICE, and still … nothing. Finally, she said I cannot increase your prescription or you will grow hair on your chest.

Now that would really put the kibosh on any extracurricular activities!

She said, and I quote: "You just need a man!"

Another stop was a trip to the drug store, not for a refill, but for other "precautions" since the doctor had informed me sex had changed a lot in the 35 years I had been out of circulation.

Well, the sex itself might not have changed, but the precautions were not to be ignored.

It was not like the wild sex days of the '60s. No, now people actually took precautions, and not just to prevent pregnancies.

Oh my!

So this is how I ended up at Walmart in the health products section looking for "precautions," not having a clue where to find such things, and who do I run into?

None other than Eduardo, the handsome Latino I met at last month's chamber mixer. He was younger and very handsome.

Ok, he was hot, I admit it. (Maybe that cream was starting to work.) I had been seconds away from asking a clerk for assistance, and luckily had not yet mustered the courage to ask, when Mr. Eduardo appeared on the scene!

We chatted for a while and once he exited the store, I wiped the sweat off my brow and found the necessary provisions.

This pointed out to me that now I really needed to work on making time in my busy life to date. I had been evaluating my work activities and deciding which things were actually worth doing.

Being your own boss and working on a commission basis has its advantages and disadvantages.

Advantage: you don't work 8-5 for someone else.

Disadvantage: you don't work 8-5 for someone else.

Hence, you're never off work and constantly trying to figure out how to make money.

The time crunch had hit. If I was ever to meet anyone, when exactly would I be able to connect? Let's see — how about next Tuesday, from 10:00 to 10:15 a.m. for coffee? That was it!

Now it was time to get real! I was not going to have a relationship with anyone on that schedule, except maybe the mailman. Something would have to give.

If this is important enough to pursue, I would have to figure out how to make time to date.

But one last thing. There was a procedure I considered - and am still embarrassed to admit considering: facial fills.

After careful examination of this old face, I realized I looked like a puppet. You know, the marionette type where the jaw drops and moves. I had those same lines! They even have a name for it — "puppet mouth."

OMG!!

I called just to inquire … "It's usually about $500 is all."

Is all??? I'm on a budget here. But I still went for a consultation.

"Oh no, you'll need more. Plan on $1,000." Yikes! Can my credit card handle any more? After the separation, I still had mounds of debt to pay off.

But I really wanted a date. I mean, really, really wanted a date.

What the hell. OK, schedule an appointment before I chicken out.

Then the time arrived for the procedure. The procedure that would make me look younger and more beautiful - so even I could get a date.

I knew it wasn't really going to do all that, but it should make some improvement, right?

The technician first started up on my cheek bones. I mentioned I wanted the "puppet mouth" done, not the cheeks, trying to sound like I knew what the hell I was talking about.

"Oh no," she replied, "We do the cheeks, and it stretches the skin so the lines by your mouth smooth out."

OK, well, she went to classes to learn how to do this, so she must know what she's doing.

Anyway, "If we just fill in the lines by your mouth, then you'll have 'monkey mouth,'" she replied.

Great. I get to choose — monkey or puppet —which do I prefer? I just kept repeating, "All I want is a date."

If I get a date, this pain — physical and monetary —will be worth it.

Well, $2,000 later, after two trips, the only difference I could see was my credit card bill. It just kept growing.

I took bunches of photos, which are still on my phone. (Great way to practice selfies, by the way.)

Seriously, I could tell no difference at all.

But it worked — just not how I thought.

Soon after the pain in my face diminished, although the pain in my wallet had not, my friend from college returned my call and left me a message.

Yes, he wanted to see me. He'd like to take me to dinner, and he hesitantly mentioned my ex (because he didn't know we were divorcing).

When I called back to reply, I mentioned the tiny detail that it was just me now.

We had a lovely time. First time I ever went on a 7-hour date! He thought I looked wonderful, although he wouldn't have known the difference anyway. After all, it had been 30 years since we had seen each other.

He was a perfect gentleman. He ordered wine in a bucket. No one ever did that for me before. I was impressed. He even paid for dinner. (I know, I don't get out much.)

We made plans for another date and another date.

My confidence grew. It felt good to be out with a man, especially a man who liked me. I even thought, gee, it would be nice to hold hands. I missed the touch of a man.

But something held me back. My instincts said it would send the wrong message.

He was a good friend, but the passion was missing. I didn't want to hurt him by giving the wrong impression. It was clear after awhile, he wanted a LTR, and I had wanted a DATE, nothing more. (For those of you who haven't spent a lot of time on dating sites, LTR means "long term relationship." And DATE means just a date.)

Now what? How do I get out of this gracefully?

I told him he'd never meet the girl of his dreams if we went out all the time. I shouldn't monopolize all his time.

So I begged off a few more invites, and before you know it, I was finding other guys to date and keeping busy with GF's and other activities.

It was a great experience, and I'm glad I got back in in the dating game with an old friend.

Chapter 16

Looking for Love

Only in the last two years did I learn about the movie, *The Secret*. After watching the movie and listening to the audio version, I began to think about how you can create what you want in life.

Then I learned about a book by Arielle Ford, called *The Soulmate Secret* and started reading it. I decided to try her suggestions so I could attract the man of my dreams.

In order to find your soulmate, you need to first make a list of the qualities you desire. That exercise in itself is a real eye-opener! My first list focused more on physical attributes and not as much on other attributes.

I set about following many of her suggestions. The main focus was believing I could attract my soulmate.

At first, I didn't think it was working as I kept meeting guys in the strangest situations. In retrospect, I realize they ALL were very much wanting to get married. This was one of the top things on my list!

The Universe does give us what we ask for.

I was meeting guys who wanted a wife, who *needed* a wife. (Sounds a lot like the husband who left.)

The other physical characteristics they didn't necessarily meet. They were all tall (also on my list) and perhaps the eye color I specified, but most had grey hair.

After all, it's pretty hard to find a blue-eyed, dark-haired man, 6'3" to 6'4" aged 55 to 65. At that age, they are lucky to have hair … at least on their head.

My list was, well, unrealistic. And it didn't really have the right attributes on it.

You can't find what you want if you don't know what it is.

One of my GF's suggested I didn't really want to get married … I wanted to have fun. I hadn't even thought of that! I'd only thought I just needed a new husband to replace the old one.

Really, that wasn't the case. I was tired of picking up after someone else, cooking/cleaning for them. I wanted someone to go places with and do things with – the part of a marriage I'd been missing.

I wanted the fun, not the work!

What a revelation.

I followed many of *The Soulmate Secret* suggestions, like making a romantic corner in my bedroom with a vision board, red candle, heart-shaped plants and pictures of what you want in a mate.

I had two pictures of men who adored their women. Yep, that's what I wanted - a man who adores me.

I even cleared out half of my closet, one nightstand and one chest of drawers. There was even an empty stall in the garage for his car.

I was making room for the new man in my life, whoever he was.

It was time to get clear on what I wanted in a soulmate/BF/Significant Other. I decided to take a week's vacation, alone, to a quiet place where I could "think" and not be distracted touring or visiting the sites.

It sounds ridiculous, but I'd never taken such a vacation.

I packed up the dogs, my painting supplies, a bunch of romantic movies, and food for a week and went to a rustic cabin on a nearby lake. If you've seen the movie *The Choice*, I was aiming for such a romantic getaway on a waterfront in North Carolina.

But since I lived in California, I opted for Huntington Lake. Alas, there was no love of my life in the cabin next door as I had hoped.

Nevertheless, the time spent there was one of the best things I've EVER done.

It is something that should be done regularly, possibly yearly, to keep one's life on track.

I have to admit I did work while there and found I could work remotely with little effort AND still make money. It was definitely something to consider. I might not have to be tied to a desk to make a living.

I spent time painting, swimming, going for walks and enjoying nature. I watched squirrels and wrote poems. I made a fire in the pit each night (the only time I missed having a guy around), drank wine, ate when I wanted and what I wanted, including pancakes, fried eggs and bacon, filet mignon and au gratin potatoes.

I watched romantic movies. I watched to be entertained and instead I got educated.

How did I know which guy was the right one in the movie, *Far from the Madding Crowd*? It was PASSION!! Yes, passion was the missing ingredient.

Watching the movies led to updating/revamping my soulmate list. Item #1 was PASSION.

Other important attributes were:
Family
Integrity
Hard Working

Listens to Me

and Can Take of Himself!

Physical attributes were no longer so important, although I still prefer some hair "on head," as I put it. Doesn't matter the color. You get the idea.

I was now looking for a mature man, an equal, a partner, someone to enjoy life with. The deleted items included – "someone who wants to get married."

At this age, unplanned pregnancy is not going to happen, and I'm not looking for a sugar daddy (not that I'd find one anyway), so marriage wasn't really the point. It wasn't a necessity.

My new list was updated as soon as the car was unloaded upon my return.

Ten days later, I met the "one" … or so I thought.

Janie Jurkovich

Chapter 17

Finding First Love

I don't know what possessed me to check the dating app on my phone, as I had stopped daily check-ins due to hopelessness, but I did one afternoon.

The pic was of a bunch of people, not a guy. Before I swiped it, I looked at the person's first name and the company which showed up in the first line.

Oh, that's my new tenant's company. I read more.

OMG! It was my tenant!

I had met him the previous month when he toured our building. I don't usually meet the tenants unless I lease to them directly. In this case, the other agent said his client wanted to meet the owner.

"I'm busy," I had thought. "Just send me his financials and the lease."

All business, that's me but I went anyway.

I was late to the meeting; no surprise there. I didn't wear the ring on my left hand as usual because I was going to an event right after where I might meet guys. (Wishful thinking.)

We were talking about the building. I asked about his business and made a rather smart-ass remark about why was he moving to our area in that business as we already had plenty of those.

I wasn't even looking at him. I was really being an impatient jerk. He happily replied that there was enough business to go around.

I looked at him and his twinkling eyes and smile and immediately knew he had read *The Secret.*

I was stunned because I knew virtually no one who had read it. And this was an item on my updated Soulmate list: "Someone who has read and understands *The Secret.*"

The next thing I did was check his left hand – no ring. I looked away and got back to business. He signed the lease and later moved in.

But I had no clue he was available and looking until he showed up on my dating app.

I swiped right.

Holy crap! It's a match! What do I do? I had 24 hours to text him or he was lost forever.

OK, so I texted but what the heck do I say? "Hi, do you always go for your landlords? Are you looking for reduced rent?"

No, I wrote something else. He wrote back!

We set a meeting for 4:00 p.m. that day. It was convenient as it was near my office where I needed to get the mail anyway.

I had a dance class that night, so I wore shorts with a long top even though we were meeting at a bar/restaurant. No need to impress him; the real me doesn't wear a dress and heels all the time.

The "date" went well, although it felt more like a job interview when I thought about it later. Luckily, I didn't think like that when it was happening or I would have freaked out! I was just talking to someone I already knew briefly.

He gave me all the stats (I guess that's what you do now). He was married 4 times, divorced, 6 kids, 2 step-kids, various business jobs, some college, etc.

I don't even remember what I said.

He showed me a pic of him and his extended family including ex-wife, her husband, all the kids and wives and 8 grandkids (so far).

Well, he must get along with his ex. Kudos for that. He's not a deadbeat dad. And he must have learned something if he's been married before, a lot.

He's got initiative and drive. He moved to a new town, alone, to set up a business. I know how hard that is when you move with the military, and we had a support system.

He looked good to me. He even walked me to my car and asked for a hug. Gentlemanly. Asked for a kiss. Real gentlemanly, but I misunderstood and went for another hug. (Dating dilemma when you wear a hearing aid.)

He said he'd make time to see me. And he did. This was nice.

Next was a two-hour lunch. Feelings were developing. Sparks and attractions were growing.

Yikes, a real kiss in the parking lot? I can't do that. OK, I'm a prude. The thought of a 60-year-old making out in a parking lot is not good. It is a scene I would not want to witness, let alone participate in.

What the heck do people do nowadays? What the heck did we do in the olden days? It's been so long, I couldn't even remember! Even though I wanted to kiss him, I was scared shitless.

Being in public only made it worse. My gosh, someone I know could witness such an atrocity. I mean one of my partners works across the street. He might go to lunch there.

Can you imagine him saying, "Oh, hi. How's the lease renewal going on the building? What are you doing making out in a parking lot in broad daylight, you hussy you?"

This was my imagination and fear taking on a life of its own. We'd better find another place to make out (or whatever it's called nowadays).

The next day I received a cute text about how many minutes his apartment was from my office, just in case I wanted to meet for a kiss.

I took the bait later in the week.

Again, I was scared to death. I had only kissed, really kissed, one man for over 3 decades. What if I forgot how? What if I didn't like it? Worse yet, what if *he* didn't like it? What if it's a mistake to be alone with him and I'm in over my head?

The rampage of doubt raged in my head, but the desire to be kissed by this man, had me shoving the doubt out of my head. Only positivity raised its head. It felt like the right thing to do.

I could tell he was a nice guy. He was definitely worth taking a chance on.

The connection was strong, and it wasn't just because I wanted a man's touch.

It was like a dream. Everything was perfect. I literally felt I had died and gone to heaven. Every word, every touch, every brush with his lips, the long deep kisses. His respectful demeanor. All were perfect for a first-timer like me.

I muttered, "Don't pinch me. I don't want to wake up."

Long lunches were full of conversation and sharing our life history, hence the need for long lunches when you are our ages.

It felt great to get to know each other better. Sometimes I found myself staring dreamily in his eyes with no idea of what he was saying.

"Okay," I would say to myself, "Focus and pay attention or he'll think you're a dimwit."

It was difficult, but I put up a good face.

The connection was fast and kept getting stronger with every encounter. Sure, I had dated quite a few guys before my marriage.

But nothing, NOTHING was ever like this!

It soon became apparent something was very wrong/different/unusual.

I was daydreaming while driving, hitting curbs and barely staying in the lanes. I left my cash at the market when getting groceries. Try explaining that one to the store manager!

My mind was elsewhere. But where?

It certainly wasn't on work. I was so scatterbrained, I couldn't concentrate. I was making zero deals. Translation: zero money. A scary place if your income is mostly based on commission and you've got a huge house payment and no one to help with expenses.

It was time to figure out what the hell was wrong with me. So I did what any other reasonable person does, I Googled it.

The answer was clear.

I had all the symptoms.

OMG. I had fallen in LOVE! Yikes!

Now what?

On a scale of 1 to 10, with 10 being the happiest, I had already been at 10. I was happy — very happy — after coming to terms with the life changes of a marriage dissolution.

Regular gym workouts had increased my reading to an 11 with all those feel-good endorphins.

Now? I was a certifiable 12, totally off the charts with endorphins. It felt like I was on drugs, not that I know what that's like. Well, maybe legal drugs like they give you after back surgery or a hernia operation. It was even better. Again … yikes!!

The analyzer in me reasoned — well it's nice to have some attention from a man, someone who cares for me (or at least puts on a hell of a good imitation), someone with whom there is a wonderful connection.

Okay, it was pure bliss. Needless to say, my confidence soared. And yet … not quite all the way to the top.

Doubt was creeping in.

Friends had mentioned the three-date rule. After three to four dates the rules changed, and the stakes changed. The expectations change.

Oh no … not that!

Holy crap. The thought of someone seeing me naked was a scary thought. It's one thing to even think about whether you want to go to the next level, quite another to think what that entails.

Not just the "precautions" my doctor adamantly suggested. (Isn't that an oxymoron?) But the biggest worry of all – do the parts still work?

I was afraid of being like the tin man in The Wizard of Oz. (Only 60-year-olds can relate.)

Did I rust out from in-operability?

I heard visualization was a good way to get through a stressful, new, uncomfortable situation.

Eventually it would come to this. You can only have so many "third dates" before the guy figures out how to count, even if he's slow.

Well, visualization wasn't going to get rid of my extra 20 pounds, so I opted for camouflage versus throwing something in his eyes causing blindness.

Time to find a negligee.

GFs tried to help me find something that looked sexy, not trashy, and had proper support where needed. Who knew this would be so difficult?

The last guy (my ex) didn't even notice if the flannel PJs had feet in them or not. This guy might notice, so I better step up my game.

OK, now to strategize how to "slip into something more comfortable," like they used to do in old, very old movies. That seemed more plausible than ripping our clothes off. I needed time to turn off the lights.

All the worry was for naught. The feelings were there. The connection was there. My one-word description would be "magnetic."

It was much, much better than any visualization I ever had.

The only glitch was during an embrace when he tugged on the

negligee like he was trying to unzip it or something (and there was no zipper).

"I don't think it does that," I murmured.

"No, it's the tag," he replied. Apparently, I had forgotten to remove the price tag.

Well, at least he knew I hadn't been sleeping around.

Now, a reasonable person would have seen a few red flags.

Multiple marriages, enough children for a softball team, ex-wives still in the picture, work commitments, a home base in another state, and health concerns. (Like, who wouldn't have them with all this on their plate?)

From my overly optimistic view, these were just circumstances to embrace. After all, anyone over 50 has at least some baggage. Even folks like me who lived under a rock for decades had baggage.

Nevertheless, our time spent together was wonderful. My face beamed. People routinely mentioned that I looked really happy. I never felt happier, or couldn't recall when.

Still, I kept waiting for the other shoe to drop.

And just when I felt it was safe to "pinch me" and I wouldn't wake up from a glorious dream, the other shoe dropped.

We were planning to go out that night after having gone out the night before. I texted him that afternoon and said "bring your breakfast shake" because I assumed he was going to stay the night like he had before and I would be eating my usual Sunday bacon and eggs.

He texted back to say he'd be heading home after dinner.

He needed to focus on his health so he wanted to "curb extracurriculars" until he felt better. He hoped I would understand.

I didn't feel like I was getting dropped. But after that, it became more and more clear that I was an "extracurricular." He was always busy with work or his health care when I reached out.

I was sad, but happy at the same time. Sad because those red flags seemed to present too many obstacles to my guy that he felt he had to step away for awhile. Happy because I had discovered that I could be in love again.

It was time to reflect on where I was now.

I've been in love and with a man other than my ex. It was glorious.

I'm no longer afraid of a relationship with a man. I know what a mature man looks like. I know somebody thinks I'm beautiful, sexy, and smart. Somebody likes kissing me, and I definitely remember how much I love sex! I feel confident in my own skin again.

No one's going to take that away from me, EVER AGAIN!

Sounds all good to me.

I truly felt like I had done this dating/semi-relationship thing, and I could do it again. I can get back on the horse again. Mmm, maybe that's not the best metaphor. You get the idea.

I can do this! I can have a happy life. I'm stronger than before. Revisiting the past was no longer in my thought process. It was full steam ahead!

Chapter 18

A New, Better (Much Better) Life

With the divorce all but finalized, it was time to truly move ahead.

I reflected back on where I started – afraid, demoralized, embarrassed, broke, worried, used up, discarded and confused. It was not a very good place.

But now, the world was opening up to me in ways I never dreamed possible.

My saddest moment had led to my rebirth. I was set free like a butterfly, ascending from a cocoon.

Once I learned to embrace the challenges and look for the lessons, coupled with a positive outlook, the world unfolded before me.

I was transformed like a dragonfly into a happy, beautiful, strong, sensual, loving creature, devoid of hurt and pain.

Life was joyous once again!

Poem

A Life by Default

Are YOU Living A Life by Default?

If so, maybe it's time to take a stand.

I refuse to live a life by default. A life where decisions are made all around me. By someone else.

Where I am a victim of circumstance. Like a tree blowing in the wind. Hither and fro. No control of its own.

I refuse to live my life under someone's down-turned eyes and up-turned nose. I refuse to live up to another's definition of what my life should be. I refuse to revert to the default position. I refuse to tell myself, "Oh well, it isn't meant to be."

I refuse to live a life of default.

I'll scream it from the rooftops till my voice is hoarse. I'll tell whomever is listening, but I only need to convince myself.

It's MY life and I will take charge and I vow NEVER to live life by default.

Janie J

Afterword

This was not — and won't be — the end of my adventures.

It was hard to go through all of this and sometimes I can't believe that I'm telling you this, much less putting it in print!

I hope you got a few laughs and tips (always remove the price tags!) from my experience.

But the slight embarrassment is worth it to me if you can feel like you're not alone and that you too, can get through whatever it is you're going through, whether you're single at 60, 30 or maybe even 80!

Now that I'm well on the journey to living the life I have imagined, I'm on a mission to encourage other women to live the life THEY have imagined.

I write about my lessons, failures and victories on my blog at JanieJ.net.

I've also written and published two books: "Live the Life You Have Imagined!: Simple Ways to Begin Living Your Best Life" and the "Live the Life You Have Imagined! Companion Journal."

I speak to women's groups and share more stories and strategies from my ongoing journey. Contact me through my website (JanieJ.net) if you have a group that would like some encouragement and inspiration.

I never imagined that I would do all this. (I probably should go back and revise the title of my books!)

You can do it too!

Janie J

Made in the USA
Columbia, SC
11 August 2020